OFER EVEN

DIGITAL POWER
TO
THE PEOPLE

*A Guidebook to Reducing Consumption
Without Lowering Your Standard of Living*

Digital Power to The People / Ofer Even

Translation from the Hebrew: Ziona Sasson
Contact: ofer@heu-law.com

ISBN 9781546345190

Table of Contents

INTRODUCTION

A corporation's most powerful weapon is doubtless its marketing, which assails us from nearly every angle: newspaper headlines, threats of a "recession," and countless blatant and hidden ads that encourage us to consume yet more—far more than we need, and usually for much more money than we can really afford to spend. To fight this onslaught, we must take one simple step: become familiar with ourselves and our needs while getting to know the "enemy" and its desires and weaknesses. Corporations are interested in more money—our money—and in more power—the power with which we endow them through nearly every business transaction we carry out.

If we take a moment to look around us and review our

personal histories, we will discover that we are capable of maintaining a rather high standard of living without stretching our limits. From a purely economic point of view, this of course has several advantages, many of them long-term. If, for example, we save money rather than put ourselves in debt, we will be able to use these savings in the future to meet our real needs and fulfill our real dreams, the ones we want to make come true, and not those the system has brainwashed us with. We will be free to choose.

It is very helpful to consider money like we consider time—that is to say finite—and manage it accordingly. For example, if you're thinking of going to the gym before work this morning, you will have to prioritize, get up an hour earlier, postpone some things to later in the day, or maybe even to tomorrow. There is no time bank from which we can draw a few more hours to add to our day. If we perceive money in this way, we will begin to make better decisions.

An especially simple series of actions will return consumption control to us. The following guide is even for those among us who have no interest in actively battling the corporation world, but simply want to live their life quietly and peacefully.

IT'S CHILD'S PLAY

OBJECTIVE: TRAIN YOURSELF AND YOUR CHILDREN TO OVERPOWER ADVERTISEMENTS

The game I play with my children is called "Who is selling you, what and where?" Begin playing among yourselves (the adults) and then include the children.

You could be on a car ride with your family, riding the train, sitting at home, out at a restaurant or in the movie theatre. All perfect settings for the playing of this game. The objective is to identify "who is trying to sell something, what and where."

The first stage calls for the most basic, most intuitive identifications: billboard signs, newspaper ads and radio and television commercials — what I consider classical advertising.

You might see an Ikea sign inviting you to buy a new bedroom set, or an ad for the latest Mazda model. There could be a catching sign that tries to persuade you to buy a comfortable armchair. Or, how about a highly sophisticated vacuum cleaner, or just simple interchangeable colored panels for your coffee machine? All these things score you points.

You can actually mark every ad in the newspaper, count every promo on YouTube or tally television commercials. Review what the ads are trying to sell and who stands behind each ad with your children.

The second stage involves hidden ads. For example, when you go see a movie at a movie theatre, ask your children or friends to identify commercial products that appear in the film as if by sheer chance. For example, an Apple iPhone, a pack of cigarettes in the lead actor's hand, a cool sports car, a Coca Cola. It doesn't really matter. The same searching can be done of YouTube clips.

You can even distinguish hidden ads in the newspaper

and on event talk shows. For example, an article devoted to healthy eating can actually be an advertisement for a food company. A TV special on a group of tourists in Paris could actually be attempting to coerce you into buying an attractive vacation package right now. The examples are endless.

The third stage of the game involves detecting all the brand names you see, then analyzing them together. Why do cars need different emblems? What is the purpose of that? What is the difference between them all? You can explain to your children or friends that the emblem creates a desire for the product, it creates in us a sense of identification, togetherness, status, separation from the herd—these are basic, still fake values of most corporations. Over and over again, they try to create for us a sense of freedom and uniqueness. It is an illusion.

The strategy is clever. It brings me to believe that, if I am driving a Mercedes, I am rich. If I have an Audi, I have status, and my life is given more value. This differentiation between products increases my desire to consume more and more. Imagine a world without brand names. Just a machine that goes from one place to another. After all, what do ninety-nine percent of the people really want? To go to work and get home safely at the end of the game. Nothing more.

According to the latest statistics, a person in the Western world is exposed to nearly ten thousand discrete advertisements over the course of one day. We are bombarded every second from a different angle, without even noticing. Billboards on the way to work, direct or hidden advertising on the radio, endless ads and marketing items in the newspapers, and so on. The goal is very clear: to increase consumption, to increase one's subjection to companies and their products, to increase one's debt.

The more methodical among us may challenge their children to figure out which giant corporations are behind each produce, masked by or labelled as belonging to small or medium-sized local companies.

After a few months of playing this game, after you and your children and friends have become fully aware of what surrounds you, and of the unending attempts to sell, comes the final stage, which involves the advancement of a single question: "Do I need what they are trying to sell me this minute?"

The moment you reach such a level of awareness at

which you question whether you really need that coffee machine that does acrobatics, that special peeler for melons, that pair of shoes that helps you "walk on the water like Jesus," or that cool apple slicer, you have already stopped the barrage. The very fact that you are applying common sense and distancing yourself from the brainwashing that is advertising—that is a victory.

If you decide that you do need that specific item, you then ask a subsequent question: Will I be using this item a year from now, five years from now, ten years from now? As soon as we apply these tests to every product, we are less prone to overconsumption. We begin to understand where we stand, and, most importantly, we learn how to reduce spending without any real harm to our standard of living.

SORTING

OBJECTIVE: TO DEMONSTRATE JUST HOW MANY USE-LESS ITEMS WE PURCHASE

This exercise is simple. Open all the drawers and closets in your home. Go over all the items stored away there, and make a list, with total honesty, of which items you have used in the past two years, and if you felt their absence at all during those two years. It can be books, clothing—shirts, shoes, accessories—kitchen utensils, or dish sets you once bought with the idea that, someday, you would be hosting a meal for three hundred people. You may also find electrical appliances that you had bought on a special sale and are still in their original packaging, unopened.

A good friend of mine, Mark, who completed this exercise a short while ago, discovered a bunch of items of which he had no recollection: a robotic vacuum cleaner from the previous year that hadn't been used even once, an electric shaver bought five years prior that hadn't barbered a single hair, a sophisticated electric screwdriver that lay forgotten in the basement, twenty-five floor rags that were bought when he moved to his new apartment eight years prior, two sets of trays and a stash of summer shirts—exactly what' s needed for the cold Canadian climate.

Mark's discovery: most of what he'd stored away in his closets remained untouched, and could have been nonexistent altogether.

This exercise can and should be carried out every few months, but hopefully doing it once will succeed in teaching you there is no reason to store things in your home that are not used regularly, and there is certainly no reason to buy them in the first place.

You're probably saying to yourself, "Wait a minute, if most of the things cluttering my home are unnecessary, perhaps that's the reason that I need to move to a bigger house with more rooms, more closets and bigger storage areas! Is that why I rent a storage space, that is to say a cemetery, for all the purchased and saved items that I never use?"

Perhaps, after sorting through your belongings, you may discover you are living in a house whose capacity is filled by things you don't need.

Yes, I know. Nostalgics will immediately defend the shirt they've saved from their first date, the teddy bear from their first Valentine's Day, an antique empty perfume bottle—I'm sure the list can go on! My advice, put aside some items for nostalgia's sake, fix them in a box, and, five years from now, open the box to see if it contains anything you've looked for or missed. Most likely, the answer will be "No." So, why not simply photograph the items? You may find that a picture is more than enough to satisfy your wistful sentiments.

DIVIDE INTO THREE

HOW THE WORLD OF THE CONSUMER IS STRUCTURED
AND HOW TO SAVE

As a consumer, there are things you "need" but don't "want," like dental insurance/visits, life insurance or car insurance. I can safely assume that no one has a strong desire to have dental work done, no one really enjoys having teeth pulled. But, there isn't much you can do; if you need a root canal, you need a root canal. In this realm, advertising abuses fear through the exploitation of superstitions and anxieties. It is a very aggressive marketing world, as it too addresses different levels of consumption. You could sold a very expensive insurance plan in case your grandmother catches a child's disease, or a highly costly home protection policy in the event a volcano erupts on Fifth Avenue. Here, too, it is about choices: I don't need car insurance if I don't have a car.

The second category includes things you "want" and "need," following Maslow's Pyramid—from food and a place to sleep all the way up to self-fulfillment. Here, too, the range is large and facilitates a wide variety of consumer habits. A fifteen hundred square foot apartment isn't enough for you? That doesn't mean you need a five-acre estate. The city's public transportation system isn't adequate? That doesn't mean you have to buy a Maserati or a Porsche.

Let's consider who really profits from these purchases. For this category, the advertising is more sophisticated. It doesn't aim to frighten us, because there is nothing to fear. It attempts to convince us we really and truly need that Maserati or that Porsche—that we really must buy that plot of agricultural land that may be re-zoned as residential in the next millennium; that we definitely need that loan to buy – what?

The third category consists of things you "want" or "really want," but don't "need." I used to call this category the "shopping channel" category. Today, I call it the "eBay" or "Amazon" category. You see an amazing piece of equipment or diet plan that guarantees the six pack abs of which you've always dreamt. "Wow," you say to yourself, "I really need that." It could even be a special coat rack or vacuum-seal storage bags for linens. On eBay and Amazon today there is an endless variety of chargers, loudspeakers, dinosaur-shaped cookie cutters or concealed LED lights for the clothes closet, you can buy anything.

Ever heard of "big eyes" syndrome? For those it affects, your eye grow bigger than your budget.

This category represents goods that will lie around your house, collecting dust—the very same goods you discovered you've never touched in the last exercise. It may seem like these items are inexpensive or even cheap, yet, for this reason, we buy so much their low prices become irrelevant, and they add up.

For these things we "want" but don't "need," companies push special buttons. They work on our desires, they sell us our dreams, they give us status. You want these things to feel more important, to be noticed by others, to dazzle people with your success, money or power.

If we revisit the previous exercise, take everything we have and divide it into two piles—one pile consists of the things we use routinely, the other of things we haven't touched in a year—we will discover that the pile of things we haven't touched is at least four times bigger than the pile of used stuff.

Do you sort your clothes? Do this, and you will discover that your daily wardrobe formed of just a few items. The clothes you've purchased specifically for themed parties, or special trips you're yet to take—those are the clothes you don't need/use. Had you needed them, you would have worn them.

All you've done by purchasing these unused or not-often-used items is help the corporation that sold it to you get richer. You've boosted the wealth of the gods of consumption without really elevating your own level of happiness, which was your goal, and which, in the end, is totally unconnected to basic consumption. Perhaps for one single moment while shopping you felt you achieved something. But, what did you achieve? We've all been brainwashed to believe that if we have that one top or just those jeans we will be more attractive, we will fit in, we will be smarter, taller, thinner. We will be more of everything.

The last category, which is no less important than the previous three, include those items for which we develop an unhealthy obsession. The contrast between our desire for a certain item and its actual use value should teach us a lesson. If you have developed feelings for a certain product, a red flag should signal danger in your head.

Fixation on a product with a price you can't afford needs to be confronted, and, no, buying it is not considered addressing the issue. If you have such a consuming passion, you should immediately question, who is really gaining from the purchase? Why do I feel like i need this to be happy? Sometimes, we shop and buy things to compensate for or cope with certain personal issues we're experiencing. Unfortunately, marketing agencies capitalize on this as well.

Many studies have demonstrated how the layout of supermarkets has become a science, formulated to cause us to buy more – the height of the shelves, the fragrances, the location of different types of products, it is all calculated. An entire field of specialization for planning and designing supermarkets has flourished to encourage consumption. This includes computers that monitor which areas of the supermarket people spend the most time in and in which areas the least time, to move stimuli via fragrance and color from one place to another. It is these stimuli that create our desire to shop.

In a world in which we are constantly competing with others to be more successful, richer and more attractive, we inevitably consume things we don't need.

The described games and exercises are meant to create within us a new conscious, independent awareness, totally disconnected from the monstrous marketing machines that attempt to define beauty, success and happiness according to their products. This awareness will lower our level of consumption, augment our savings and return control to our own hands.

One of my biggest dreams is to create an app through which all our shopping will be monitored and regulated. The moment we are about to run out of or use up a certain product, the app will alert us to go out and buy that product, and that product only.

Like your car's gas gauge, the app would compute all our consumer products so that we would only be urged to buy when the gauge is close to empty. We will then discover that we have been consuming most products in huge amounts, analogous to towing a gas tank behind our car (which increases the gas consumption...), instead of just filling the tank when it is nearly empty.

When all of us, through systems such as that of this app as well as self-disciplinary tactics, dramatically lower our acquisition of goods, we will no longer be bound to the corporations, to debt. We will be independent, we will be able to work less and devote more time to ourselves and our families, to friends, to things that are important in our lives. That is how we will gain happiness—not from purchasing another cellphone, another wardrobe and another car, for which we long momentarily, and which provide us with pleasure even more ephemeral.

TO PAY IN INSTALLMENTS OR NOT

THE GOAL: TO LEARN THAT OUR DEBT WILL NOT DISAP-
PEAR IF WE DON'T PAY NOW

A few weeks ago I went to the local supermarket, picked up a few basic items and went to the cashier to pay. The total cost came to $27.97. Almost instinctively, the cashier asked me, "Do you want it in payments?"

I looked at her in surprise for a brief moment, then said, "Sorry, I don't have that disease." This is my traditional response to such a question, and it catches the cashiers off guard every time. But, why should it surprise them? Either you have enough money in your bank account to pay for this purchase or you don't. There is no maybe having the money or sort of having the money. When we pay our bills in installments, often while also paying interest, it doesn't change the fact that we still have to pay at one point.

Every week I see people shopping at the supermarket, purchasing food that, a week later, will most likely be rotting in their refrigerators, still they agree to pay for those items for the coming six months. What do I mean by this? I am talking about credit cards.

Credit card debt is ever-increasing. If you buy a television and pay in twenty-four installments of fifty dollars each, and a month later you buy another item for twelve separate fifteen dollar installments (and so on), you will wake up one day at the beginning of the month to see that you are paying thousands of dollars to your credit card company. Do you even remember what you're paying for?

This is a contagious disease in which credit card companies and their partners, corporations, are interested in us catching. Conceptually, the mechanism seems clear—we all want to lower our upcoming payments to make things easier for ourselves, to postpone the deadline. Actually, we feel like we're buying things we don't have the money for! Sounds too good to be true, because it is. And, so we enchain our future by daily consumption of unnecessary things.

I am not in any way preaching asceticism or frugality. I am the last one to recommend people sleep on the floor, eat bread with salt and drink just tap water. Absolutely not. I am, however, suggesting we engage in smart patterns and habits, such as Shopless Friday, which I will discuss further on.

If, in addition to increasing awareness, people can also decrease their consumption by, let's say, twenty percent, rather than increase it from year to year, as most do, we can create a better world. This will free our money for savings, which will enable us to break out of our "debt" chains and implement real changes in our lives. Another possibility, no less attractive, is to make do with a lower income and work fewer hours, so we can use our time for other activities, such as spending time with the people we love. Our level of happiness will not change one bit. It can only rise.

SHARING IS THE NAME OF THE GAME-
OR: COOPITALISM

Okay, so you've sorted the entire house, and you are left with a huge pile of books, clothes, furnishings, kitchenware, appliances and gadgets no one needs.

What do you do now? Where should all this stuff go if not your closets? Ask the corporations and they will persuade you to sort the pile and send it to recycling, thus behaving "responsibly" toward the planet.

I say, perhaps instead of recycling, share with others. Most items in that big pile are good enough to be useful to someone else who needn't spend any money to purchase them.

Share on internet sites, on second-hand sites, use charitable organizations that deliver furniture to needy homes. What you can't manage to give away online, place outside your home on the sidewalk, and you will be surprised to discover that most of the items will be taken by passersby.

By sharing, you are helping to diminish the circle of sales, the circle of bondage.

I visualize an app which enables you to share any item you don't need, even food, by the press of a button—as simply as you share something on Facebook or retweet on Twitter.

Until such an app is created, we can decide to begin sharing, together with our neighbors in our building or on our street.

How? It's simple. Look at the items you have in your home that you use perhaps once a year or once every few months. There is that lawn mower, camping equipment, folding chairs for when you will host two hundred people, folding tables, car roof racks, bicycle racks, Karaoke systems, portable lamps – the list goes on and on.

Now imagine that there is a common storage room in your building or your neighborhood, in which all these items are stored and there is also an app through which you can reserve whatever items you need, in advance. And think again, why did we buy hundred power drills, hundred screwdrivers and hundred lawn mowers?

Now let's take a look at the future and at the trends that can already be identified, trends which the corporations may not necessarily be happy about.

If we think about housing, do we really need such big homes, which serve as storage space for the countless items that we don't need? Couldn't buildings be built with smaller apartments, but which have joint laundry rooms, play rooms, television rooms?

Cars – in an era when Google's car is covering millions of miles without a driver, it is easy to see how we are moving towards a future in which all vehicles are shared, driven by a computer, and each one of us who has to go from point A to point B will order an available car closest to his location. Why buy a car and spend all that maintenance money on it, if I only use it for one or two hours a day?

Let's continue and imagine sharing the means of production, factories, agricultural land, agricultural equipment - an extension of the models of AIRBNB and UBER. With such sharing, much more efficient use of resources will be achieved and payment will be based only on actual usage. Or how about mutual insurance of large groups of people, networks that enable mutual loans, without the banks' control; sharing by using Blockchain – digital money, or any other effective future invention for the general population.

I can already imagine those who will jump up, encouraged by the corporations that fear consumption will decrease, and yell - Communist, Marxist. Let them yell.

As I often say to those around me, Karl Marx missed by two hundred years. Today's technological era enables, and will enable with increasingly greater force, people to free themselves of the deceptive, false consciousness and influence life itself.

I am not promoting enforced equality for all. Each individual can act and guide his own journey, his life. However, by increasing mutual sharing we are applying one of the major keys to consumption that is looking far into the future and understands that the resources on Earth are limited.

A USER GUIDE FOR PROGRAMMERS OF THE REVOLUTION

VIZ. INSIGHT INTO THE MATRIX

INTRODUCTION

If we asked the world's citizens who controls the population, most likely the responses would be divided between "The President/Prime-Minister" in First World countries and military forces in the other countries—that is, if we first invalidate responses such as "my wife" or "my kids" or "my boss." In reality, however, over recent decades, and more so in recent times, the response should be totally different. It should be: corporations. Yes, those very same fabricated organisms, figments of people's imagination, during the past several centuries.

This sounds conspiratorial, almost paranoid. After all, today we are more in control of our lives than ever before. Freedom is at our fingertips, and every day, every hour—we exercise that freedom anew. Sometimes even more frequently. Thousands of small decisions every day, which we and we alone make.

But is that really true?

What we eat for lunch, the drinks we choose to drink, the ice-cream we decide to have for dessert, the shampoo and soap we use in the shower, the gas we buy for our cars, our cars themselves, our computers, cellphones, even the food we buy for our pet cats or dogs— everything, without exception, is purchased from a corporation. You can't escape it.

And, not only do we buy everything from the corporations, but we feel that, due to the wide variety of options out there, the endless choices between one unnecessary item to the next, we are free, because "it is we who make the choices." Actually, not true at all. Rather, we are led like a herd down the paths of life.

Proctor & Gamble, Unilever, Pepsico, Cargill, Kraft, General Electric—to the average person, these names mean nothing. If we add the names Apple, Philips, Nestlé, Mitsubishi and other more everyday names, one may sound familiar. Regardless, they all share one basic trait in common: they are all giant multinational corporations, each one of which has a network, more complex than a spider's web, what with subsidiary companies and ownership structure.

We will discuss the issue of free choice with respect to the corporate world later on, and clarify whether it is we who really make the choices, or someone else determines the choices we have for us, similar to how we narrow options for our children: broccoli or spinach, the red shirt or the blue shirt, Cartoon Network or Nickelodeon.

The first concept, which accounts for how we actually serve corporations with every "choice" we make, is simple. You eat Ben & Jerry's ice-cream, one of the most popular brands of ice cream, you contributed another dollar to the monstrous firm, Unilever. You buy Bonzo dog food or diapers for your baby, you paid Proctor & Gamble. You wanted a quick dinner, so ate at McDonald's, you just enriched not only this American food corporation, but also Cargill, the corporation that produces many of the ingredients that eventually go into McDonald's food.

The second concept is more complex. If the corporations control us, who controls the corporations? Who is the person or what is the entity that can, by will, shut down the computers, the machines—who can pull the plug and send all of us to a dark and disturbing world? An even more important issue and challenge is how we prevent that person or entity from doing so. Is there a way of stopping him/it at all, or is all lost?

A different question can also be posed: how can this centralization be dismantled? How do we change the way in which money is distributed around the world. How can we change the fact that one percent of the population holds ninety-nine percent of the money, and one hundred percent control over the lives of the greater part of the world's citizens?

It is asserted that no single person controls these corporations. My way of looking at it —and every creationist who believes that man was created by God will disagree—is that human beings have been evolving for over millions of years, as held by the Darwin's theories. We come from several cells that, with time, developed and turned into the complex creature called Man.

Our progression has been so complex that, several million years ago, at some stage, a mind and a soul evolved, a certain vibration that connects all the atoms, neurons and protons, and it alone can manage and operate the complex assembly called Man. Thus, we have the modern human being with a soul and dreams and longings, along with a destructive nature that can cause total annihilation.

I believe corporations progressed in the same manner, beginning with limited companies that were formed to serve people, which later, at some stage, a mind and a soul evolved. The being has a growing, opportunistic soul—and not just one that powers the "invisible hand" as economists have said these past centuries, but one that exploits endless hands that are no longer invisible in order to control and manage not only businesses, but all of us.

This description of the corporate soul is not a metaphor. Like Descartes's dualism that separates body and soul, the same applies to the super-corporations that have developed a soul.

Such is precisely the reason why there is no one person culpable—there is no one person who can decide to pull the plug, take the money, disappear to a secluded island and let the world go to hell. The corporations are programmed by the corporate soul to create a mechanism that increases consumption and profits, by which more power and money can be amassed. Whoever refuses to adapt to these goals is sent to the fields of eternal frost and glaze where there is certainly no money, and nothing can grow.

So, how do we beat the system? To do so, one needs to understand this mechanism—this soul—and attack it at its weakest point(s). Like David and the smooth stone, he drew from the brook to shoot at Goliath's forehead. Like Neo, who destroyed the Matrix by controlling his consciousness. In our case, it is not about the few versus the many. It is just the opposite. They are the few. We are the many.

In this guidebook I will explain how these corporations grew, make clear what allowed/helped them to become stronger than any government in the world and, most importantly, seek points of weakness in the corporate soul, a Trojan horse of sorts, that the corporations themselves created out of their desire for more power. I will also endeavor to show you the immense power of we, the people of the modern world, which, if systematized, can bring down these money tyrans. I will also provide actual tools with which you can resist corporate brainwashing and the daily organized attack on our minds in this guidebook for the fiscal revolutionary.

But, wait. Why do we need to fight them at all?

One of the first things a doctor does when someone states he has been long suffering from a variety of inexplicable symptoms or disorders is question the person's emotional state.

"A healthy mind equals a healthy body" is a basic tenet, dating even before New Age theories and religious movements. One's state of mind has significant impact on the body. When the mind is unwell, the body suffers, too. In religious terminology, this is referred to as "the soul."

It is safe to say the corporations are ill. They are controlling, greedy for power, hungry for money, predatory, aggressive and they turn men into doormats using their sheer scope and power. They, the corporations, the aggregate body, are sick, because the corporate soul is sick.

And, because the soul is sick, the corporation turns

into a sort of cell that has lost control, and has begun dividing itself into more and more sick cells. Like you know what. And, now the body has no choice but to fight back, even though it is defeated and in a position of submission, like the ant who has been overcome by the tomentella fungus, which has led it to the precise tree trunk it needs, in order to destroy it and grow out of its head.

To a certain degree, we are all zombies, creatures whose heads have been stuffed with increasingly more information, all of which is meant to serve the corporations. We are all figuratively drugged with information and opinions. We all serve one and only one objective—to increase consumption that will lead to greater profits. We are that same ant I mentioned above, and the corporation is the fungus that is growing in our heads.

Now, let us stop and look around us.

IN THE BEGINNING....

Apple, Google, Nestlé, Pepsico, Wrigley's, Proctor & Gamble, Coca Cola, Intel, Berkley's, J.P. Morgan, Unilever, Merrill Lynch, Goldman Sachs, Capital Group, General Electric, Cargill, Philips, Mitsubishi—the most recent studies indicate that less than one hundred and fifty corporations are running the world. Some of these control us absolutely. We are practically addicted to them, without knowing or sensing it, if only because it never crosses our minds that we are addicted, and "an inmate cannot release himself from prison."

Proctor & Gamble, for example, produces and/or markets, directly or indirectly, a wide variety of products, from medication and toothpaste to fashion accessories and even food. Every few months this corporation purchases another company, and then another, and, thus, enters different consumer areas and grabs another chunk of the market.

This makes no difference to the small customer. He gets the same products, part of the same misleading sales that actually serve only the corporation—for, by definition, every sale that leads us to buy more of the same product actually turns us into storage units. Instead of keeping products in supermarket refrigerators or storage rooms until they spoil, we store them in our own homes until they spoil. And, then we throw them out.

Unilever holds an endless network of companies that produce basic food items, ice-cream, beverages and skin care products. Again, all we do is repeatedly buy the same product, when, in fact, our money, which historically supported small companies, or even medium and large-sized companies, is now financing a monstrous corporation.

The first corporation in the world, the Dutch East India Company, was established in 1602, long before globalization was initiated. The idea of a corporation stems from the Latin word "corpus," meaning the creation of a body that is separate from the people who have created it. In a way, it is similar to the Golem created by the Maharal of Prague, who was given his independence. The goal of the first corporations was to preserve their monopoly over the Asia trade via permits to establish companies that were under Dutch control.

Clearly, those companies were completely administered by people. They received their mandates from kings or governments, that is, from the sovereign powers of the sixteenth and seventeenth centuries. In 1896, the change began in England, with a court judgment in the case of Solomon vs Solomon, considered till today to be one of the most significant judgments in corporate law.

Solomon, a pleasant and clever man who owned a tanning business, decided that he wanted to turn his business into a company. However, by British law, one needed seven shareholders in order to establish a company. Solomon tried to outsmart the system and registered his wife and five daughters as shareholders. Nine hundred and ninety-four shares were held by him, and the six remaining shares were divided amongst the rest of the family. Solomon was also the major bond-holder, bonds that he bought against his property. Thus, he had created a new legal body that had precedence and priority over other creditors.

When his business failed and the loans he took from the other creditors were not returned, the latter filed suit against the company, fearing it wouldn't meet its debts. In court, Solomon claimed he had priority in receiving monies as he was the major bond-holder. The creditors, on the other hand, claimed what we claim each time a tycoon asks for a "haircut"—he was simply transferring money from one pocket to another, yet the money remained with him and therefore they were the ones who should get precedence in returning the loans.

"It is a travesty of justice," they yelled. "He is using legal sophistry to avoid paying his debts."

In that world, prior to the era of corporations, Solomon lost in all the courts, even though, as the main bond-holder, he was an insured creditor. But, he didn't give up and took his case to the House of Lords, where it was determined that the company was a legal corpus separate from the stock owners, therefore there is nothing to prevent Solomon from receiving his money before the other creditors, as Solomon and the company were not one body.

That is how the first corporate-like persona was formed and separated from the physical being of the owner. That same persona, as an outcome of the court judgment, can commit itself, take responsibility upon itself and sign contracts. And, in regard to legal disputes, it is a persona separate from the person(s) who established or run(s) it. As such, it is not a physical being, but rather a social construct, created by people, an illusion that exists in everyone's mind. The company owners, the creditors, the courts—all is nothing more than an illusion.

The next stages of corporate development came, of course, during the era of revolutions—the revolution of print, the industrial revolution and the digital revolution. All these together eventually led to globalization, resulting in the evolution of local companies into giant global companies that exploit the cheap resources of one country in order to sell at high prices in another. It is happening today on a large scale, just as it did the Old World, where products are sold for a high price whilst the production workers themselves receive hardly anything at all.

From that point on, companies continued to develop into super-corporations. The ability to separate the owners or directors from the legal corpus, the company, turned the entire business venture into something far simpler and more rewarding. But, as happens in the business world, the Golem is quick to turn on its creator at the first opportunity. The entire operation eventually boomerangs.

Up until nearly twenty years ago, stock holders still had control of the corporation, and the Board of Directors served as a form of super-administrator. There was a CEO who led the corporation down a chosen path, and there were also owners who stood at the head of the entire system and filled their pockets with money. And, then the corporate soul was born.

WHAT EXACTLY IS THE SOUL?

As I see it, the soul is a product, the result of the development of a critical mass of cells. Like the amoebas in prehistoric times. When we were but a small amount of cells, there was no need for a soul. The mechanism worked without thoughts, without inner supervision. But, slowly we developed and evolved into more complex organism. When we reached the tipping point, the critical mass from which the human soul was born quickly separated from the matter that comprises the human body, and that is how separation came about between the body, which takes up physical space, and the soul, which doesn't.

In Star Trek, perhaps the most successful science fiction film series in history, it was possible to translocate someone from one place to another. Captain Kirk, standing on the launching pad, would instruct his chief engineer, "Beam me up, Scotty," and be instantly transported to the starship, Enterprise. My personal interpretation of this scenario is that, in the very progressive world of Star Trek, the secrets of the human soul were decrypted in a manner that enabled translocating the soul together with the physical body.

It is actually about the dualism of the human body—the physical body on the one hand, the soul on the other hand. Many philosophers and researchers in the past discussed, contemplated and wrote about the unity and separateness of body and soul. In contrast, there are the hard sciences, such as physics, biology and chemistry, and, based on known purely scientific facts, and certainly according to the Physicalist philosophers, we are composed of many different formulas, both simple and complex, of chemical compounds and biological processes. Matter, nothing more. The soul, from a purely scientific perspective, does not exist, as its existence cannot be proven.

Even though my point of view places me on a certain religious scale, I definitely believe that the soul is external to matter—an invisible and inexplicable shudder that causes matter to arrange itself, to move, to act, to become a soul that does not take up any room in space or in time, that cannot be perceived through any one of the known senses—whose existence cannot be proven by math or science. Yet it is entirely there. And it is completely separate from us. Do you wish to call it a soul? Does it exist simply because we can imagine it? Whatever. It doesn't really matter.

The exact same theory applies, in my eyes, to the corporate world, perhaps even more so. The same process that unfolded in the human body hundreds of millions of years ago took place in an especially accelerated manner in the corporate world over the past few decades. Somewhere along the way, when a critical mass of money, power, flow of knowledge, data and organizational skills formed, that same soul that administers body and matter was born.

The initial practical significance of the corporate soul is that there is no one single person that can press the red button and bring darkness upon the world.

What does it mean?

As regards a normal company, the man or woman with

control, the major stock-owner, apparently can still shut down his/her company if he/she so wishes. But, let's look for a moment at the one hundred largest financial bodies in the world—this ranking is ordered by turnover—according to Forbes in 2014; thirty-seven of these entities are corporations: Bank of America, Chevron, Walmart, Google, Apple, etc. Each of these companies realizes a turnover of hundreds of billions of dollars per year, with tens of thousands of employees and worldwide activities. They are owned by stock holders from all over the world, most of whom have no connection with each other. The great majority don't even know one another. The point is there is no single person among the stock holders or at the executive level who has the power to end a corporation's operation.

The ability to generate virtual money and power, composed of the binary numbers zero and one, facilitated the birth of the corporate soul. If I own a company that runs a grocery store, I can wake up one morning and decide to shut down the grocery store. If I am one of sixty-million shareholders of a certain corporation, however, the endless number of the shareholders and the complexity of management and operation of the company at an international level disables me from acting individually on the corporation. At that point, the corporation has a soul, and makes its own decisions. It is, in fact, the brain that activates the invisible hand, a theory that has turned into reality and has taken control over it.

Personally, everything became clear to me the day Steve Jobs died, passing on to another world, all gadgets and cellphone chips of the fifty-third generation. Instead of Apple sinking into disuse or collapsing, its corporate soul (which was unrealized while Jobs was alive) immediately emerged and preserved the framework.

This is not a metaphor. The corporate soul, in my eyes, is absolutely real, and, as such, has only two interests: accumulating power and accumulating money. These are meant to serve the corporate soul in order to generate even more power and more money. Endless, infinite. Like the businessman in The Little Prince who is constantly involved in counting the stars that he is certain belong to him, and with which he wants to purchase more stars, and so on. The marvelous writer, Antoine de Saint-Exupéry, in fact defined precisely the corporate soul: it wants to grow and grow and grow, boundlessly. Money for the corporate soul is like the universe to humanity—as of today, we believe it has the capacity to continue expanding without end.

If a corporation's CEO works to advance the will of the soul, the Board of Directors will reward him/her, buy him/her a yacht and add dividends to his/her already huge salary. He/she will be surrounded and sought by big-name people, eat only the finest and most exclusive foods in the world and get drunk off the most expensive wines and liquors, and fly to private islands for vacation. Whatever it takes.

But, if this same CEO doesn't work to advance the corporate soul, he/she will be replaced immediately. No emotions involved.

The Board of Directors, which seemingly runs the corporation on a regular basis, also enjoy luxury when the corporate soul is indulged. Its members fly all over the world on their private planes, receive very high pay for their minimal work and live the "good life." If, for even just one moment, they question the basic objectives of the corporation, they too will be replaced, as if they had never existed.

Outwardly, serious business people claim the shareholders control the corporation. However, in reality, the controlling interest in the giant corporations is generally very small, not more than two to three percent of the company's shares. Just to clarify, one person can gain control of a large corporation because of great dispersion of shareholders in listed companies, even if his direct holdings are significantly lower than the required fifty-one percent, via a control pyramid. In a control pyramid, shareholders that leverage the little money they have by setting up a holding company that establishes additional companies, and, each time, issues less than fifty percent of the stocks to the public until it accumulates enough money to purchase the controlling interest in the corporation.

Further, the shareholders, as long as they are working in the interests of the corporate soul, will gain a great reputation as setting the way and leading to success. However, if, for example, they decide to be environmental and contribute a high percentage of the profits to environmental projects, or, as Jewish tradition dictates, contribute ten percent to charity the corporate soul will either: 1. Lead to a takeover by an alternative group of shareholders, usually through hostile means, or 2. Simply commit suicide by dismantling the company and selling it, in parts, (and, yes, the invisible hands as well) to other corporations. Thus, the separate parts in which the corporate soul is intertwined can merge into new entities and carry on the fundamental goals of corporate life, which are to accumulate more power and more money. Always more.

Of course, we don't mean suicide in the human physical sense, but a corporation that doesn't succeed in finding alternative shareholders has the option, just like humans, to willfully end its existence. The corporation can simply choose to be dismantled, opt for Chapter 11 (of the American Bankruptcy Law regarding the management of a company's bankruptcy, providing certain protection from creditors), or be sold in parts to other corporate souls. That is, to begin planting seeds and growing somewhere else.

The development of the corporate soul was made possible by the digital revolution. Over the last twenty years, the connection between real money and virtual money was severed. If, up to the beginning of the digital era, there was a link between the amount of money in circulation and the amount of gold in the bank vaults, or the amount of physical assets the amount of money in circulation is now completely exponential. All it takes is adding another zero or two or a billion, with the stroke of a keyboard.

Every corporation has the potential to create unlimited

value—trillions of dollars that enable it to continue increasing its money and power without end, regardless of the quantity of resources on earth. Perhaps because, paradoxically, money and power, which happen from knowledge, are the only infinite resources on earth today. What are they actually worth? We shall find out.

Since corporate souls have two interests—power and money—and care about nothing else, they operate efficiently and quickly to attain their goals. While they are quicker and more flexible than any government in the world, corporations have also become more powerful, because governments, by their very nature, are plagued by bureaucracy, which hinders the quickness and efficiency of procedures.

Corporations, via a network of lobbyists, and mainly by buying off people, can move between countries at top speed. For instance, if regulation is imposed in China, they will emerge in Africa. If they are limited in the United States, they will set up shop in Ireland. They will immediately hire regulators who just have ended their position in the public sector, with no cooling-off period. And, sometimes, in especially corrupt instances (that is, corrupt according to the public, not to corporations, which traditionally lack common ethicality and morality), even while these regulators are still partially employed in their previous positions.

What regulator would dare oppose a company capable of providing him, his children and his grandchildren with future employment and a high standard of living? And, if he can be brave enough to oppose, as few courageous regulators have done, who says he won't be fired immediately?

Since money is disposable for corporations, they can use it to generate more power and control with which to exploit the lack of coordination between governments, the bureaucracy and regulations, and to create a situation of "divide and rule," which only produces even more money and power. The secret of perpetuum mobile deciphered.

These acquisitive corporate souls have secondary goals, which obviously benefit their main goals. They seek to subjugate all mankind—to be the producer or the consumer—so as to accumulate more power at the people's expense, and deepen their bondage to the corporate machine. The formula is simple: An enslaved person is incapable of seeing the big picture. He is only interested in preserving his standard of living. Meanwhile, he is completely enchained by the monstrous system of marketing and brainwashing.

The corporate souls have invented for themselves a god, similar to humans. Their god, however is technically a bountiful one, as is He who belongs to Christianity. Yes, the god of the corporate souls is the god of consumption. As absurd as it sounds, this god is also the god of the modern world. The god of governments, the Maker of economists, the Lord of simple people who don't understand anything about the production, consumption, and transfer of wealth aside from what they're told.

And, what does this high and mighty god of consumption instruct us to do with his imaginary book of rules and regulations? Increase consumption to increase growth. Increase your debts, so that more and more money is yielded to the greater system. And, the more your debt increases, the more enslaved you are, because, simply put, you belong to the creditor. To clarify, the more you're in debt, the longer is your sentence.

You take out a loan to cover a previous loan, and then yet another loan to cover the previous, previous loan. You take out a mortgage to buy an apartment, then you take another mortgage to cover the first mortgage, in order to upgrade your home. This cycle, which is almost impossible to break, has only one victor—the corporate soul(s).

It may sound like a conspiracy theory, but corporate bodies truly control the entire digital system. They control search engines, such as Google, as well as all the PR firms and advertising companies throughout the world. They control, or used to control, information (more on that further on)—that is to say, they control why and what people are exposed to, what is important, what is desired. We have created a monster, and it controls us with incomprehensible, blinding force. The Golem has risen against its master.

If Adam Smith's invisible hand didn't have a name, now we can give it both a name and a face—the corporate soul.

WHERE ARE THE REINS?

The process that began almost accidentally, thanks to the stubbornness, or perhaps stinginess, of the friendly Mr. Solomon, has reached a point today at which computers and machines have outstripped humans. The corporations have grown far greater and stronger than the population. And, there is no single body in the world today who can take on the corporate world alone—that includes governments as well as the people who outwardly run the corporations. It is still not too late to take control over the situation, but we have already suffered significant losses, and must act quickly before the issue reaches the next level, after which only violent confrontation will bring about change.

To what do I refer?

In a prospectus from their earlier days in business, Google staff wrote a sentence that became the company's unofficial slogan: "Do no evil." Unsurprisingly, this sentence has been erased from the company's code of ethics. My feeling is that this sentence was spread as a warning—it is best to limit the power of corporations, as the corporate world ferments evil. And, ironically, to this world Google went! Because there was no other way. The merger of power and money by its very nature creates monsters that just want more and more. If money makes the world go round, the entire world will follow the footmarks of money.

In his science fiction writings, Isaac Asimov defined the three laws of robotics: A robot will not harm a human, nor allow by default to have a human harmed. A robot must obey the orders of the human, as long as they do not conflict with the first law. A robot will see to preserving his own existence and welfare, as long as this does not conflict with the first or second laws. Later on, another law was formulated and placed before the other three: a robot will cause no harm to humanity, and will not allow, by default, that humanity be hurt.

But, in the corporate world, which certainly, from a philosophical viewpoint, generates a form of sophisticated automation, these limitations are totally lacking. Corporations are moving forward quickly without ethics, without morals, without boundaries or limitations. They operate purely in accordance with two basic laws, which I've mentioned already: accumulate more money, accumulate more power. These laws are observed in practically every step taken and every decision made by each corporation. Money, power, money, power. Left, right, left, right.

Even if a corporation claims to follow rules and regulations, its influence and authority are so great that it can easily change rules, bribe regulators and, if necessary, migrate to countries with less restrictive laws.

The cleverest and evilest initiative corporations can take is to persuade a person to increase his/her debt. There seems to be nothing more harmful to an individual than irredeemable debt. When this happens in the grey market—where interest rates are so high that returning a principal loan is impossible, and one is constantly trying to meet just the interest payments—we complain and demand a police investigation. But, the corporations legally, and in most cases without usury, apply the very same tactics.

Even though it doesn't serve us in any way, we are constantly told to increase our debt and increase our commitment. Take out a loan, pay by credit, pay in installments, even for lower sums of money.

Why?

Corporations want us to chain ourselves further to the production line of work, of modern slavery, to which we are bound, and from which we cannot be released.

This idea to increase spending has been pressed into our minds, discharged through clever tactics and covert advertising, such as newspaper items on "Families in Economic Growth" or "The Right Economy." Sometimes, could even be more simple than that—a product shown for a second in movie, or a casual remark uttered by a public figure, or an apparently pointless viral video that sweeps the net.

The corporate soul and those who serve it want us to continue believe the more we increase our debt, consume and divide our credit card payments into installments, the better our situation will become. Corporations promise that, by extending the scope of consumption, the world economy will grow and flourish, and we too shall benefit.

Hold on a minute.

Even if this theory is correct, who is it that benefits from this growth? Let's assume, though it is totally irrelevant today, that our income will grow by ten percent every year, and, as a result, we will be fit to increase the scope of our consumption—to buy another car, buy more brand name clothing items, perhaps a new smartphone. Who will benefit from all this increased spending? You guessed it— the corporations.

How does it work actually?

Let's say you go to a movie theatre and on the screen runs an ad that makes you want to purchase a state-of-the-art piece of technology—which is the "cool" thing to own. In other words, on the screen runs an ad that makes you want a product for which you have no need. Without the ad, you wouldn't have ever considered buying this imaginary item, even if you saw it in a store. But, after seeing the ad, you say to yourself, "Hey, I really need that!" or "Boy, that's something I've been wanting to buy for a long time."

Our minds are programmed by corporations to constantly live in the future, thinking always of our next car, our next cellphone, our next shirt, what we plan to buy or eat on a certain day. We are all slaves of consumption.

The corporations skillfully create in us a feeling of deficiency, a sense of constant privation. If we don't have the latest name brands, we are unhappy. We truly feel that we need those brands, and the kind and well-meaning corporations so generously supplies us with them.

The way corporations succeed in brainwashing us so completely happens basically from their historic control over several sources of information. More importantly, here, in the realm of information and knowledge, lies our opportunity to fight the corporate souls.

FROM THE TOP OR FROM THE BOTTOM?

Until very recently (that is, historically speaking) knowledge throughout the world of information coursed in a pyramid shape, and from top to bottom. Ahram from Cairo. Pravda (Truth) from Moscow. Even the Weekly Address of the President of the United States via Radio. The ruling powers have always decided what information would reach the public. Before the digital era, the king would send his message out to his subjects via his heralds. These messages would reach even the most remote areas. For the citizens of these kingdoms, this information was always considered most reliable.

Whoever held control—be it a prime-minister, a dictator, a king or a nobleman—was also the one who controlled the flow of information to the masses. If he so pleased, the sovereign would make information public, and if he felt it was, for whatever reason, to be private, he would conceal the information. No one could decipher between the actual truth and fabrication or manipulation, or as we call it today, Fake news.

This is also how knowledge functions in history books. We don't really know for sure whether or not what Josephus Flavius wrote and described was absolutely true. It doesn't matter. He was smart enough to document and to write, and his writings outlived others. This means Flavius was teller of his own story, and clearly there is no one left from that era to dispute or deny his claims.

This authority over information gave rulers and the kings limitless influence over their populace. Therefore, chances of a revolution were very remote. Such is why the sovereign powers lasted far longer than they do today. There was no one to present contradictory information, no World Wide Web to surf for answers.

Somewhere in the seventeenth century, about one hundred and fifty years after the first printing machine was invented and the start of the ensuing revolution, the first newspapers were published in Germany and then in England. In both cases, the newspapers expressed the sovereign rulers' points of view—the information simply became easier to disseminate.

The masses, before the digital era, were unable to react. They could, of course, demonstrate and shout in the village square, but this was quite fruitless. Most of the people were given to brain-washing, or what Karl Marx defined as false consciousness—the proletariat believes its situation good because all it hears is how terrible is the alternative.

This is what happens when information flows strictly from top to bottom. Today, this goes on in North Korea and, to some extent, in China and Russia. However, it also occurs in what appear to be perfectly democratic countries. Take Fox News, for instance. Many Fox viewers know no reality save the one showed on The O'Reilly Factor and Hannity.

The era of radio and television didn't change the picture. The tycoons who owned the media controlled the information that reached the masses, and each media platform served its owners and their interests. With time, these platforms turned into tools in the hands of corporations that understood power that lies in controlling the media.

But, that is coming to an end. The most significant revolution for the public is the digital revolution, which has been unfolding in the past few years, with the amazingly fast development of the internet, and the transformation of all the familiar models of the flow of information and power. No longer does information flow from the top to the bottom. It path has grown erratic.

Today, information is received at the same time from many directions, and each person chooses his/her own direction. However, we are not quite free, because the large social networks are part of the corporate world. We are, however, getting closer.

Using Facebook, for example, anyone can become a journalist and share information or judgments at the press of a button. Scroll through your news feed to find opinions, views and news, as they are all over the social media site. Still, despite our capacity as users to generate and disseminate this info, we are not completely in control of Facebook as a news/knowledge reference. Through different algorithms, Facebook has the ability to control what content we see.

With Twitter, you can be more selective in following and allowing yourself to be followed, and, thus, you can choose users with diverse standpoints so as to feed your knowledge. Yet, some say this too is about to change.

The emergence of forums, networks, such as Darknet, and sophisticated chat apps that operate on a Bluetooth platform (a feature which so far prevents the ability to track users) also enable the transmission of classified information without any supervision or control from above. Such chaotic flow of information lets people react and express themselves freely. The first seeds budded during Arab Spring at Tahrir Square in Cairo as well as at the onset of the Occupy Wall Street movement, which launched in New York City in September, 2011.

The absurd detail is that Facebook and Twitter, that is to say the corporations behind these two sites, are seeking to accumulate even more power by enabling the chaotic flow of information, the same flow that can eventually bring about their downfall.

From time to time they introduce manipulations to help us decompress and give off steam without actually taking action and heading into war or struggle with the corporate soul. If such indeed does happen, corporations will create obstacles and limitations to undermine the offensive of the masses. We can either give in or develop more sophisticated models and continue to subvert the machine.

For example, Fire Chat App allowed communication Via Bluetooth, between masses of people that can be initiated without any controlling or censoring algorithm. This is one of the few technologic platforms under no corporate control. People all over the world are beginning to find that corporations impact freedom of expression. An example—because Fire Chat was used at the huge riots in Hong Kong in 2014, the Chinese government was unable to prevent the transmission of information amongst the demonstrators. It is quite plausible that, right now, there is a Chinese corporation working to develop a form of technology that will successfully control information these types of transmissions.

Across the world today is a giant competition among corporations, each interested in developing more and better technologies that will generate more power and money. Concurrently, the chaotic dispersal of information (made possible by the advancement of technology) allows the masses or individuals of the world to express themselves and have their voices heard.

As we've seen, this development in technology has also brought about new issues for governments. For thousands of years information was transmitted through manuscripts, proclamations, books and, in recent centuries, via radio, films and television. As I mentioned above, until not very long ago, a governing body told its citizens what to think and thus was able to secure its sovereignty for many years. If a citizen did not align with his leader's doctrines, he was erased from society.

Leaders also used to assure no form of media broadcast detractive opinions. Today, any and every politician can put on a silly hat and run from one talk show to another for ratings. A modern prime-minister or president has no control of the party's jester, even if he is causing harm.

Before the dawn of the corporate soul, the change in the flow of information and the digital revolution, governing bodies controlled the media and had direct access to money and power sources. Leaders could enact specific policies and decide that their parties would carry out certain actions. Information travelled from the government downward.

Take Parliament members, for example, who were

forced to follow their party head (prime-minister or president) and embrace his viewpoint, as he held access to the media. He was the one to be interviewed, he was the one with the weekly or monthly radio program and he delivered reports to the nation. All other party members were inessential. The public was hardly aware of them.

These party members knew that the success of their sovereign would guarantee their re-election. They had to remain united and transmit the chief's ideas in a unified manner, otherwise they would have no chance to progress or keep their positions. The spotlight was not on them. The one controlling the spotlight's direction was the prime-minister, or the president, or those in control of the media.

Also, at this stage, prior to the digital era, companies were controlled by people. There were no corporations or corporate souls that could overrule governments. Governments could embrace certain tasks or ideas and follow them through over a long time period. They had the ability to declare, "I am now building the Chinese wall, I am implementing very huge projects, even if we enjoy their benefits only in another ten or fifty years—even if it is only our children or grandchildren who will benefit."

And, how were they able to do this? Because there was no political price for the difficulties along the way. The various forms of media were theirs. There were no dissenters.

In the past fifteen years everything has changed. Someone, or perhaps the corporations (without intention), changed the rules of the game. Because the path of information is now erratic, because every elected official can receive direct media exposure and wants to receive the most direct exposure to guarantee his re-election in the next primaries, the historic 'glue' holding together political parties has been lost. The mechanism of control and governance of the democracies has dissipated.

As a result, corporate souls have grown stronger than governments. If Larry Page had, at any time, invited a senator to talk the same day and time that senator was summoned to the White House, I can guess where that senator would have chosen to be.

The power and livelihood of ex-public officials lies in the hands of corporation companies and, even more unfortunately, in the hands of the corporate souls that dominate the government and their current officials.

In such a reality, most political parties see no point in maintaining long-term strategies. They are all busy getting maximum media exposure in the shortest amount of time. Instead of the classic and ideal case of leadership—in which the leader delineates policies based on long-term strategies and ideals in which he believes—the leadership is like a weathervane. The leader says what the public wants to hear, or what he thinks the public wants to hear, since such is the spirit of things as reflected in the social networks and public media.

What does this resemble?

The current state of affairs corresponds to a bus driver who, rather getting on the bus and looking out to the horizon and telling his potential passengers where he is heading and whoever wants to head in that direction can get on the bus, he turns his chair around to face the passengers, with his back to the road, and asks, "Where do you want to go?" He asks them not because he is democratic, but because he wants to keep his job. And how will the public reply? They will lobby for what they see in the newspapers, on their cellphones, or on the video screen above the driver's head. That is, they tell the bus driver (the leader) what the gods of consumption say here and now.

Presently, in this pre-revolutionary stage, the corporations have several forces, besides the marketing system and control over the powers that be, that impact the simple person. These forces are needed to prevent any uprising. Religion, for example, is an effective way of controlling the masses.

The corporations, too, have created "religions." Sports, for example. Corporations today control the world of sports, which was meant to be competitive and clean. Instead, they've made is something to follow, something to worship. Through their control they sedate the masses. FIFA is a kind of modern gladiator, a corrupt body where decisions are reached in a questionable manner, and whose goals are few and narrow: aggregate more power and more money for the corporations that control it. Therefore, every young child who becomes addicted to football or to a truly addictive computer sports game, is like putty in a corporation's hand.

Sports are a method of gaining control. Using sports, the corporations have us consume air time, remain glued to our TV screens and talk on and on about games and teams and trades. They make us feel like we're a part of the teams, like we can identify with them in a significant way. They do the same things to the players

They trade them like slaves, like profitable pawns.

If we look back, throughout history the possibility for a man lacking wealth and connections to the rich and ruling class to be in possession of important information never existed. The digital era enables every person from every social class to bring his story and his thoughts to front stage, and to do something meaningful with his life.

Tiananmen Square in China, the fall of the Berlin Wall, the disintegration of the Soviet Union—each of these events in itself was a small part of a big revolution that, over the years, can be turned into a flood. What at one time was a rare event has become routine today. The flow of information through the media facilitates discussion and responses by the masses on any and all subjects.

As I see it, all this is just a preview of the tsunami. And the tsunami will certainly come. History moves in circles—every government eventually has a downfall. The seemingly democratic system we live in, which, in fact, is just an oligarchy (a governance by the extremely wealthy)—will come to its end as well. It is just a matter of time.

At this point in time, most people haven't yet come to this realization. They are still being steered by the brainwashing they've undergone. Just let them lounge in a chair and get a direct infusion of that sweet narcotic – reality, the gladiator battles of modern times. From a governing standpoint, TV screens and social networks are ideal tools. Were they different or absent, it would take great military and police forces to control the masses. There would be fuller and louder city squares, and much more anger and insurrection.

The democracies are still trying to use television, and now also Facebook, to control the masses. saying, let them sit at home and click their tongues at how bad things are, eat more carbohydrates and do nothing. However, people are waking up—the circle is expanding quickly as people are acquiring tools that the masses never had before.

Each time someone claims that this or that consumer protest hasn't had any effect, I suggest he prepares to eat his words. These are but small, preliminary quakes progressing towards the great volcanic explosion that is yet to come.

For the first time in many centuries, the flow of information is such that no one has control over it. Actually, we could say that another soul now controls information—the soul of the masses. The masses can create content, react and rewrite history.

There is an old saying that, "history" is "his story." Those who recorded history were those who survived, such as Josephus Flavius, whom I mentioned earlier. But, today the reality is different. There are no clear victors. The narrative is being written by everyone. There are endless points of view and angles on every possible subject. There is no clear, single narrative. There is no single truth.

Today, people can choose to consume content that interests them, and the entire advertising world is fretting, rushing about in an attempt to halt the erosion of brainwash. As we've seen, advertising is one of the strongest weapons a corporation has, if not the strongest. The false and propagandized message that endless consumption will bring us happiness has worked in the past, and is still effective in most cases. The truth is that we keep on buying more and more unnecessary items. Still, the first cracks in the system are already visible—we, together, are beginning to understand the deceit—as is the growing anxiety of the corporations.

The chaotic path of knowledge enables a growing number of people to discover that they've been had. And facing this number of people is the corporations' huge struggle. They try to solve the issue by using anti-trends to create trends. They shoot with any weapon at hand to preserve their power. They are even trying to turn the rebellion into a trend, so as to profit from it.

But, it won't help them. The revolution has started, and, in the long run, will be impossible to control. The availability and easy access to media contents that are ad-free, the ability to record and watch a program at the time and place of one's choosing—there things are making it possible for us to sidestep corporations and their propaganda.

The next stage, following the radical alteration in the path of information, will be actively addressing the flow and path of money.

WHEN MONEY WILL BE DISPERSED?

By observing the information revolution and the digital revolution, which made the flow of information into a chaotic flow, we can also anticipate the next revolution: the radical change in the flow of money. Over the course of thousands of years, and till today, money has flowed in a pyramid-like fashion – from the bottom to the top. At the bottom, money was produced, by the slaves and plebeians, who labored for their lords and the farmers and growers in the Middle Ages who worked for the nobility, for the counts and kings.

When the industrial revolution came along, this order was still maintained, The industrial workers who slaved the hardest produced the most money, which then floated upward to the factory owners and first capitalists. Actually, till today, if one looks at the modern work places, he/she will notice that nearly all of them are operated like assembly lines —accounting firms, huge law firms, hi-tech companies, industrial companies, the film industry, television, advertising and fashion. Nearly all the work places in the modern era. In each of these, you will find the simple workers at their assembly line positions, which change from one company to the next, from one industry to the next. Yet, they are the ones producing.

How much do they actually earn?

Let's say that a simple worker's productive output is worth one hundred dollars. The boss pays him twenty dollars for his labor, and the remaining eighty dollars moves upward, up the pyramid – to the department heads, the CEOs and especially to the corporation's owners. That twenty dollars earning is just enough to keep the worker's head above water. Enough to consume more, to buy, to change his car, to go abroad for vacation or buy the latest nail polish. It's enough to buy a new handbag or the latest smartphone once a year. It isn't enough to retire on, with a decent pension, but it also isn't so low as to influence the worker to give up and revolt.

The simple worker, however, doesn't understand that he is moving that eighty percent of the profit upward to the C-suite and executive level. All the latest studies have shown that one percent of the population holds ninety-nine percent of the world's fortune. The more time passes, the sharper the pyramid gets. The money clearly flows from the floors of the plants' production halls—the once classic industrial companies and today's hi-tech firms—directly to the pockets of their owners.

It really makes no difference if you are a big-buck-earning employee at Google, eating sushi every day, moving between office floors using a giant slide, you are still chained to the production line. These chains are your debts —credit cards, mortgage, your overdraft at the bank. We are all prisoners to our debt. We are caught up in the idea that we must consume more than what we already have (thanks to the corporations), and the illusion of endless credit makes that possible.

If you earn fifty dollars, you believe you can spend sixty or seventy, and at times even one hundred or a hundred and ten dollars (in installments of course, so that we don't feel the burden very gradually). It is like the frog who was slowly baking in the not-too-hot warming pan, but for such a long time until it was too late.

We are always with our backs to the wall, facing the people around us in a sort of milieu of effective social pressure. "Look how much greener my neighbor's lawn is. I certainly want a lawn that green, maybe even more so." And your neighbor looks across at you from the other side of the street and says, "I want a jeep like that. "And the jeep-owner wants a long vacation in the Caribbean, like his friend from the next town. When we compare ourselves to those around us, we feel compelled to buy a bigger house, a bigger car, smoke more expensive cigars, to always be moving ahead. We spend more than we have because we can, because we see our debts only in the long run.

But, when we satisfy all these foolish thoughts, we become more and more chained to debt. We can't free ourselves from the production line, because we could easily lose everything we have. Liquidation, banks. We can't just wake up one morning and take a year's vacation. We are in debt.

Beginning with Adam Smith and his "invisible hand" onward, the global economic culture states, "Let's increase economic growth and consumption, for if we don't do so, there will be a recession, and recession is terrible." If we adhere to this idea, the result is perhaps an annual ten percent salary increase (best-case scenario). Now, if our salary increases by ten percent, the corporation grows by one hundred percent.

For every dollar we earn, a corporation earns ten dollars. The money path has always led upward. Every growth, every act of consumption serves those who stand at the pyramid's pinnacle. They've come to milk our souls. How absurd! When we outnumber them by so much!

In my opinion the real change will kick in when we change the path of money, though it still isn't clear how we will achieve this. The corporate soul of course will object, it will try to prevent this development with a variety of manipulations, including brute force. But, if information begins to circulate chaotically from the bottom to the top, then the time for money dispersal has come.

The first buds of change are to be found blossoming in consumer awareness, in the cooperatives, in our educated decisions as consumers where our money goes. This includes decreasing our consumption of brand names and consumption in general, and ignoring the pressure to endlessly shop. It is a decision to be made after we have thoroughly understood how the system of consumption impacts us, and who is really benefiting.

The moment a critical mass of people awakens, for the first time in human history the direction of the flow of money will change. It will no longer move only upward, but in all directions, and in a controlled and clearly defined way, bringing profit to the masses—not just to those at the top of the pyramid.

The corporate souls use their messengers and advertisers to consistently scare us with the threat of a recession. Huge headlines screaming "Recession!" in red ink with indecipherable graphs tell us that, if economic growth stops, recession will set in. Recession? That's terrible. Oh, no!

Let's stop for a minute and think about this equation.

Endless growth is based on the assumption that there are endless resources—land, energy, water, gold, oil. If our resources are limited, so is our growth. But, in reality, the only thing that can grow on earth without limit is cancer (which also kills the host in which it grows).

In the past few years we have acquired the understanding that there isn't enough land for the future population. There isn't enough water to quench the thirst of the billions of people who will populate the globe in a few more decades. There isn't enough oil to power public transportation forever. There isn't enough food to feed ten billion hungry mouths. And, when the resources are exhausted, consumption will shrink dramatically by the means earth has at its disposal—mass extinction by natural disasters, starvation and wars.

More and more people are waking up, raising their heads and starting to understand the absurdity of recession threats. If economic growth happens, and eighty to ninety percent of it benefits the corporate soul or the production lords, and only ten percent profits the workers, irrelevant to their line of work, then who will really suffer from a recession? Us or them?

Let us assume that, today, we produce together one hundred percent of production. The worker takes home twenty percent and the employer takes eighty. If there is a deep recession, let's say production will drop to forty percent, and the average worker's profit will decrease from twenty percent to fifteen percent, perhaps even to ten percent. The harm to the worker will be minor. All he need do is lower his consumption, stop buying things he doesn't need. The moment he does that, the decrease in his salary will hardly be felt, as opposed to the freedom he will enjoy from the chains of the production line.

In such a situation, a corporation, instead of earning eighty percent, earn but a fraction. And, the greater the recession, the harder it will be for the corporation to continue. Its only step is implosion if it will not agree to the new flow and distribution of money.

It won't be easy. The corporations will put up a fight. They will inundate us with threatening headlines and stories in the media that they control. They will delegate certain heads of state who are in their pockets to scare the public, to pass decrees. They will mobilize armies for wars that serve their purpose—it is public knowledge that wars cost the public a lot of money, yet provide immense profits and leverage growth for corporations, and not only for weaponry corporations.

The corporations will do everything—truly whatever it takes—to continue doing what they do well, which is amassing more money and power. However, the moment a critical majority of rebels forms, the corporate soul will fade away, and power will return to the people. Commingling the chaotic path of information with a more careful and fairer flow of money—and fostering a strong community of rebels—will lead to digital power to the people!

WHO IS RICH?

One of the theories I like to play around with is the thinking that to be rich means to be able to move forward in time totally alone. For example, the car I am driving now was considered a luxury thirty years ago, for the wealthy only. The common electric window featured in every car in the world today were considered an exclusive element of driving enjoyed only by the very rich.

Being rich helps us consume state-of-the-art technology. To be ahead of the times. To be first. The thing is, in today's reality, under the influence of the world of advertising and consumerism, all of us want to be rich, and so many of us live like the wealthy live.

The richer you are, the more independence and solitude you have. When you have money, you can have your own private garden. And if you have greater wealth, you buy a private island. When you are poor, you travel by train. With more money, you travel by plane. And if you are even wealthier, you fly business class. When you are truly wealthy, you buy a private plane. When you have no money, you go to a public beach with thousands of other people. When you have money, you buy a house with a private pool. Then you buy a yacht, and finally even a private beach.

Truly, who doesn't want to live like that? Everyone strives to be rich, because we have been told that is the goal. It is one of the main teachings of Calvinism: be rich, be happy and you will go to Heaven. For the Evangelists, it is an absolute religion.

However, if we really think about luxury, we will discover that we, the ninety-nine percent, enjoy the same things as the rich. We travel, we go to the beach, take vacations, sit in our gardens. The only difference is that, with our wealth, we are not buying ourselves isolation.

Why should we strive for this isolation? —to be alone, without a crowd, without people around us? Man, the most social of animals, is meant to be surrounded by people. However, brainwashing by corporations leads us to think that we don't want to be bothered by background noise—that we want to enjoy our lives in grandiose solitude.

So, say you are filthy rich, worth billions of dollars, but you are absolutely alone. What have you gained? Wealth is a goal, not a means. You can't possibly enjoy the way when you are totally focused on the goal. All the brainwashing of the western world that is now sweeping over the Old World—India, China, etc.—sells the illusion of utopia, of absolute happiness, of luxurious aloneness.

This illusion causes people to suffer all the way along their paths of life, up to the point when one bright morning they discover their debts are so great, they are losing. They are unhappy.

This illusion also affects people who have or seem to have great wealth. These people too get trapped in the same game. The corporate soul knows how to enslave even those who are worth tens and hundreds of millions of dollars. These people buy private islands for more money than they have, and will take huge loans to finance their purchase. They can't stop. It is a compulsion.

Why?

The pleasure we feel from everything we do in life is the same pleasure. And, usually this pleasure is intensified through social interaction. If we understand what is happening around us, the background noise shouldn't be annoying or burdensome. We don't have to be alone. We need togetherness.

So, why do corporations want us to be in isolation? Alone we are a bunch of individuals lacking consciousness ad unity. Together we are a force. Whom would they rather fight? An individual? Or a force?

Try just once not to run off into aloneness. Sit on a beach with people surrounding you, drink a beer at a busy bar, bury your cellphone and strike a conversation on the train. You will discover that behind every polite smile and averted gaze there is an entire universe far greater and more interesting than any reality show, text message or Facebook notification.

People will label this text Marxist. Well, Karl Marx simply didn't live at the right time, nor did he get the right window of opportunity. Marx's basic mistake was in stating, "Let's concentrate all the means of production together and then divide them up in a fair way."

Why was that a mistake?

The answer is simple: human nature. The moment you concentrate all means of production in one place and then choose people to divide them up, there will be a lack of cooperation by those receiving control of the means of production. They will want to seize their new power, as anyone who has experience a great amount thereof.

Not only will these people refuse to surrender their recently found power, but most will attempt to accumulate even greater power and wealth by means of that power, at the expense of those with whom they were meant to share the power. And as more and more power and wealth are concentrated in the hands of the few, oligarchies will continue to form, and oligarchs create corporations. And from these immense corporations the corporate soul emerges and takes the actual control away from them.

This is not only an economic issue, but also a matter

of justice and morality. Wherever there is economic interest, there is corruption. A small, especially telling example is the issue of prisons and guns in the United States. It is public knowledge that the number of prisoners in the United States, percentage-wise, is the highest in the world.

Why?

Because prisons are a business. Every prisoner who works and produces is part of the mechanism, creating huge profits for the privately owned prisons, which are also part of the corporate world. Who are these prisoners? Mostly Hispanics and Afro-Americans, of course. They are the "easy targets" that can be brought into the system and used to make an impressive profit.

Under such circumstances, clearly there is no interest in rehabilitation, as that would lower the number of prisoners, the number of working hands, the rate of recidivism. Less working hands means less production, which means less money. Why, then, should the corporation concern itself with justice when tens of billions of dollars are at risk?

The same logic applies to the gun lobby in the United

States. The Second Amendment of the Bill of Rights is fine and well, but the Republican champions? Allow me to guffaw. Gun corporations in the United States are among the largest corporations in the world. Every person who buys a gun strengthens these corporations further.

One would expect that, every time there is a school shooting or mall shooting, gun corporations would weaken. However, corporations don't go down that easily. At that point, PR folks and marketing firms work for these gun corporations, selling the public new reasons to buy guns: It is a dangerous world out there, there are lots of crazy people with guns walking around, so you'd better arm yourselves.

These people need a wakeup call.

Rerouting the path of information is the first step to changing this mindset, as we can teach each other and reassure each other that we the people should own the means of production. We can also alter the circulation and path of money. Contrary to what we've been taught, we do have power.

What the masses need to hear, believe and embrace

is the following statement: "He who swipes, impacts." If we act wisely and increase personal awareness each time we use our credit cards—that is, if we give thought to each purchase—we can trigger a huge revolution with very little effort. It can happen only through the force of everyone's money combined, which is greater than the amount belonging to corporations, as they feed off us.

Think of corporations as huge intestinal worms that feeds off sugar exclusively. The moment we stop feeding that worm sugar (as soon as we stop ingesting sugar), the worm won't be able to exist. It's that simple.

Let's use as an example a small but revolutionary step that could affect a significant change: Shopless Friday. Shopless Friday is similar to Meatless Monday, introduced by vegans, which calls for observers to refrain from meat on Mondays. So, why designate Friday a shopless day? Because, Friday is the day when most people go out "to shop till they drop."

The impact of Shopless Friday on the economy would be great. One might suspect that it would bring about the collapse of retail chains or harm the GNP. However, if people shop only on work days, they will purchase only what they really need. When people go shopping just to pass the time, they end up buying for one reason only: why not?

The idea of Shopless Friday doesn't mean to stop buying, which is impossible in itself. But whoever swipes his credit card, does influence the market. You can choose to purchase your food in smaller shops, where the owner is someone you know. That way, at least, those same ten dollars will go to the pocket of the storekeeper and support the lower stratum of the pyramid, instead of enriching the corporation that hires contract workers.

Awareness, which developed predominately during the modern era to awaken the masses from a false consciousness, did not exist during the Marxist era.

In this modern digital era, as information travels chaotically, we, the masses, have the tools to awaken ourselves from our false beliefs and knowledge, free ourselves from the opium for the masses, from the endless brainwashing and become aware of the flow of money. When we awaken, we will also be able to affect a change. Shopless Friday is just the beginning, one small step for a man and a large step for mankind.

RETURNING TO THE BEGINNING

As everything does, this change will begin with the educational system, which is totally enlisted in support of the corporate souls. Schools in the modern age clearly educate students to be better workers, and not to be more independent. That is, schools teach students to become the most fitting and effective screws in the monstrous machine that will control them.

Have you ever asked yourself why the schools don't offer financial education? Why don't they teach about interest? About loans? About how to balance your budget? About how to be an intelligent consumer? Apparently no one is interested in school students understanding how the world around them really works.

How did the school system even initiate in the first place? At the onset of the industrial revolution in the mid-eighteenth century Frederick the Great, King of Prussia, understood that, in order to establish greater and stronger armies, he needed disciplined, literate people to transmit orders and instructions in an efficient manner, so that a hierarchy could be created in which instructions were transmitted from top to bottom.

That is how free, mandatory education was born for children from the age of six to twelve.

Imagine...

You take children, arrange them in rows and you give them schedules to follow. You have them attend school for a specific number of hours. You have them stand in formation on an asphalt courtyard. You ring a bell when they have to go to class. You fill their heads with mathematics, reading and whatever else it takes to operate machinery on the assembly lines, otherwise you teach them to be obedient soldiers who can receive written orders and calculate with simple mathematics an artillery's range or trajectory.

This is how Frederick the Great created soldiers, how he stripped them of their independence, joie de vivre and creativity. He immersed them uniformly in the system using a single template, as dramatized in Alan Parker's film, "The Wall," based on Pink Floyd's masterpiece. We have all become obedient soldiers that serve great causes which mean less than nothing to us. The trouble is, we can't see that. Ironically, we feel independent. We feel like we have free will, when, in reality, we are followers. In sociology, this is called "tracking"— someone has marked out a track for us, leaving us no choices to make.

Today, schools continue to operate in the same manner and systematically deaden students' curiosity and creativity. No teacher really prepares his/her students for the fast-changing world, but rather for the industrial revolution three hundred years ago. Whoever demonstrates independent thinking is immediately marked as strange. The independent, intelligent students serve as "do-not" signs. "Learn from them," we're compelled to think. "They won't amount to anything, ever."

These intelligent students are the ones left absorbing all punishments and judgment. Those among them who surrender and fall in line (some via drugs, such as

Ritalin, which returns them to the comfortable, controlling box and generate great income for pharmaceutical companies) are highlighted as success stories.

If we look at computer surveys from the past twenty years we will discover that the greater part of the active work force in the United States learned computers auto-didactically, and not in school. These people, most of them in their thirties and forties, knew how to sit for hours and apply themselves, and, over a very short time period, learned material that supposedly takes twelve years of schooling to acquire.

We are told that attending school is important. It's supposed to prepare us for the world, but, in reality, we are trained to be workers on a production line where we must produce a mandatory output with the machine we are operating. And if we don't meet that output, we are disposed of, replaced by another who can meet the demand.

Back to the corporate soul...

People who work on the production lines produce and increase each corporation's income exponentially. One day it's John, another day it's Steve and the next day it's Shirley. The important thing is that the machine continues working and producing the greatest possible output. To large companies, people are replaceable. People are insignificant—merely numbers fed into the great money-making machine.

I see things differently. If we think ahead we will see that, in order to train the future generation, we must preserve childhood creativity and curiosity. We must respond to wonderment and inquisitiveness. We must not try to "cure" these qualities. Ritalin, for instance, aims to "tame" children—to put them in boxes, when, really, they should be thinking outside of boxes. But, boxes make up the system. The child must stay inside his space and not disturb the teacher or the well-behaved children around him.

Why are they considered well-behaved?

Because they are studying how to become a production line worker, and, in this process, acting like members of a production line. The system is naturally oppressive, because it has a goal: to produce more money and more power for those in control. There is a reason why Ritalin is one of the most popular medications sold throughout the world, which funnels tons of money into the system. The reason is that it produces a secondary advantage by turning creative and curious children into suppressed robots.

Education is not the only issue. Let's talk about nutrition.

In his film "Super-Size Me" Morgan Spurlock underwent an experiment. At its start, he was in perfect health—blood pressure, sugar levels, everything was fine. Six weeks later, besides his obvious weight gain, other side effects included depression, impotence and high blood pressure. Conspiracy theories, whose validity remains completely unverified, hold that following the exposure of the results of eating junk food, the most popular medications sold in the United States became medications for blood pressure, impotence and depression.

This is an obvious case of cause and effect. The corporate world will sell us unhealthy food, superficial culture, inadequate education, you name it! As long as it suits the goals of the corporate souls, it's sold. They will take any and all measures to leave us addicted to their products—food, medication, technology, etc. It is an endless cycle of consumption and money.

LONG-TERM THINKING AND THE TERROR OF THE HERE-AND-NOW

"If a man knows not to which port he sails, no wind is favorable," maintained the Roman philosopher and statesman, Seneca. The basic problem in most systems is that they lack long-term reflection. There is no home port, there is no goal. People have no reason or desire to know where they are heading and why.

And, thus, consumer culture is all about the here and now. There is no long-term view, as thinking long-term necessitates saving, prudence and caution. The here-and-now approach is "Eat, drink and be merry, for to-morrow we shall die."

That line of reasoning is why we consume one hundred

and twenty percent, or even three hundred percent, of what we earn, because tomorrow something will come up. We will win the lottery, or, in some surprising manner, get an inheritance from Grandma. Such rationale function so that we don't concern ourselves with the long-term, because "things will work out." Or "maybe, tomorrow will never come".

In some countries, this is reversed. The national security corporations create a constant sense of insecurity. They instigate threats, which end up being nothing more than campaigns built on fear intended to send us rushing to the malls to eat, shop and drink, for tomorrow we shall die, literally.

For some years now I've joked that one day we will discover ISIS is nothing more than a hidden advertising campaign for kitchen knives.

But, seriously, notice how ISIS's actions generate income for major media corporations. The public is drawn by the terror and consumes the news broadcasts, which enjoy high ratings and during which a lot can be sold through advertisements. Stop for a moment to think about what would happen if all the communications media in the Western Hemisphere came together and decided to stop giving ISIS news coverage. If you are not in the news, you don't exist.

Let's pull it back a bit. Terror as a means of increasing consumption. This is a serious tactic used by governments, political leaders, media corporations, banking corporations and credit corporations that sell us almost unlimited credit at crazy interest rates. This uncontrollable credit immediately increases consumption and triggers the here-and-now approach., it augments the virtual happiness and immediate tranquility created by the momentary acquisitions.

In the end, everything boils down to a matter of choice. But, in reality, what exactly is that freedom to choose? And do we have such freedom?

THE ILLUSION OF FREE CHOICE

From the dawn of humanity "choice" has been considered one of the most complex and crucial topics, especially in religious and philosophical circles. Is everything predetermined, as the more conservative religious circles claim, or do we have the ability to steer our lives? The deterministic viewpoint deems every human action a result of previous circumstances.

In Judaism, for example, you have a choice between good and evil. However, regarding the actual definitions of good and evil, we have no choice. In the same vein, the Calvinist philosophy, which forms the basis of American capitalism, claims that we generally have the ability to choose, and if we are good consumers who buy and earn lots of money, we will go to Heaven.

Even entirely secular philosophies define, in their own way, what is good and what is evil. So, freedom of choice is in fact misleading, considering we do not initially delineate the limits and parameters of human behavior and existence. Add to this the socio-psychological perspective that views every choice we make as the result of our total personal history, and from the moment we've made a choice we have already fulfilled our pre-determined purpose. You will realize how specious our concept of "free choice" really is.

In economics it works the same way.

One of the most familiar choice dilemmas, and one that is seemingly trivial, is the "menu" dilemma. An intelligent person enters a restaurant, sits down, studies the menu and finds himself terribly perplexed. He calls over the waitress or waiter and asks, "What do you recommend?" Later, after the main course, he once again studies the menu, this time for a drink. He calls the waitress over and inquires, "What do you have to drink?" then scans the menu some more, only to choose what he always drinks in the end. Still, throughout this event he is plagued by indecisiveness, anxiety and pressure (to a small degree).

To me, if a person is very indecisive, his choice is meaningless. If you have to choose between something that is rated nine out of ten and something that is rated three out of ten, then you probably won't hesitate.

Indecisiveness is about choosing between something rated eight and a half and something rated nine. At this point, you start to ponder and feel the pressure of decision. But, in reality, what is the difference? After all, both are really of the same quality, and, most likely, you could never differentiate between them.

So why even place yourself in a state of indecisiveness?

This example demonstrates illusion of choice. We think we are in control. Should we buy the iPhone or the Galaxy? Should we choose the Michael Kors handbag or try another designer? We are very much in control of our lives. In absolute control. But, then again, only virtually. Like in religion, all we need do is make the "right choice" which has already been mapped for us.

The main goal in distinguishing between brand names, including cars and luxury items produced in the very same plant as the less luxurious items, is to create this illusion. Except for the very few, such as super-sports-men, can anyone really feel a physical difference between a Nike, Puma or an Adidas sports shoe? Why are we so indecisive about choosing between nearly identical products which, without tags or brand labels, we couldn't tell apart. Yet, we remain uncertain and perhaps even end up buying two brand names, because we find it too hard to choose one.

The gist is that, in the end, we do not buy a product that serves our real needs. We debate with ourselves, we feel we have absolute control over our lives because it is we who decide whether to use maple syrup or honey on our pancakes. Every day, without fault, we make decisions regarding matters that are of no consequence, as if there is any real difference between the options we are debating.

This misconception of free choice leads us to acquiring goods and services in ever-increasing amounts, thus feeding the growth of the corporations that want to sell us more. We augment their monetary turnover and power. Often, we increase our own debt in order to make choices like the ones above, and we end up tied by the chains of credit to their production lines, because of our virtual choices in their consumer products. Choices that are of no importance. Zero. Nothing but an illusion.

Allow me to stop for a moment and observe myself sitting and writing.

Here I am, sitting on my balcony with a whiskey in one hand, a cigar in the other, enjoying life. If you've read this far, you are probably saying to yourselves, "Com'on, aren't you supposed to be an ascetic? Completely abstaining from consumerism? From pleasure? A spiteful Buddhist monk?"

My answer is a resounding, "No." I believe everyone must enjoy life, enjoy his existence. The trick is not to turn into a slave while doing so, but rather learn to identify what really brings us pleasure, whether it be shopping or perhaps the people around us and everything that surrounds us.

For me, I like to sit on my balcony with my whiskey and cigar, take a break from my mind, review and observe the people around me as they go about their own life journeys. I am often put in mind of the following analogy of a trek: When you embark on a foot journey—a trek—you need to make the right decisions while packing. You need to consider every location in the world, and find the right accessories for that location.

I have a metaphor looking at life as a long trek, Once you've started out, as you are walking your first mile, you observe the color of the sky, you hear the murmuring of the brook and the sound of the birds, you sense the fragrance of the flowers and you relish the people around you. Most likely, you don't pay much attention to what you are wearing or any other insignificant details.

About three miles along the trek—at this point you are at an incline—you are busy observing the group of people walking ahead of you. Another four miles and you are now focusing intently on the back of the person in front of you. You no longer hear birds nor smell flowers, you just see someone's back. The scenery goes by peripherally while you try to concentrate on maintaining a breathing pattern and a reasonable pulse, all while keeping your eyes on the man ahead of you.

Fifteen miles into the trek you are feeling the blisters on your feet, you are watching the stones on the path in front of you, trying not to fall and cursing the moment you embarked on this trek, wishing it would end. You CamelBak backpack and water bottle, your Fitbit, your

Patagonia jacket, your North Face backpack—these items are now of zero interest to you. I know quite a few people who at this point, would be willing to throw these popular outdoor items off the top of a mountain.

If we compare this trek to modern life, we will find that, somewhere around the age of thirty, we have already reached the seventh mile. What we see is tomorrow morning, our annoying wife or husband, our bank manager who phones us. Our credit cards that swallow up their income once a month, our unbearable boss who harasses us. We see a network that is closing in on us. We are no longer enjoying the journey, the path, we just want it to be over, we want to be free of it.

The greater the burden we take upon ourselves, meaning our debt, thanks to the media and the digital world and corporate souls, the more strenuous this "trek" becomes, and the less likely it is to ever end. All we notice are the blisters on our feet, the flies and mosquitoes buzzing around us.

A person who wishes to preserve his sanity would stop, open his backpack, take out his little gas burner, make himself some coffee and breathe in the clear mountain air. After sitting and relaxing for fifteen minutes, an hour or a week, he would contemplate what he has already accomplished and what lies ahead. He would stay put until, once again, he sees the sky, the clouds, hears the murmuring of the water and the song of the birds. He would then take a deep breath, filling his lungs with oxygen and look upon reality with fresh eyes. Observe his surroundings.

It is not the end that is most important, but the way there. We may reach one summit or another, or not. Regardless, we must stop, embrace, take pleasure in our journey. The summit, any summit, will most likely still remain tomorrow.

One thing people are unable to do, as they are obsessed with reaching the summit, is really take pleasure in the landscape around them, enjoy the view. The corporations hope we don't look. Looking doesn't cost money (at least not yet). The consumerism culture gains nothing from murmuring brooks and bird calls.

One day, if we don't stop and take a look around, perhaps the corporations will gain control over our landscapes and commercialize them. This is already happening. Take, for example, tourism, or the bottled mineral water we buy at our supermarkets, which was once accessible for hardly any money at all, we would drink water from the tap and felt that it quenched our thirst, it was good and it met our needs.. Corporations have convinced us that bottled water and water dispensers are healthier, tastier and will help us live longer than tap or natural water.

Let me further illustrate this for you using another analogy: You are playing a computer game, currently at the first level. There are different kinds of monsters, strange and weird enemies. Soon after you start, your character "dies." You try again and again. Very slowly you become adept at the game. And the more masterful you become, the less aggressive and bothersome the monsters seem to be. Suddenly, you're moving up in levels. The game gets hard again. You fight and fail over and over, until again you practice enough and develop adequate skills to succeed and level up.

Most people reach a point (or level) in life where they stop—they grow content. It is Parkinson's Law in manpower placement: Only if you are mediocre enough will you be able to preserve your work place. If you are no good, you will be kicked out. If you are too good, you will be kicked upward till you hit the glass ceiling, which will frustrate you until you are kicked out.

Most people are familiar with their monsters—bosses, family, bank managers, co-workers. They are not seeking to move up a level. They do not seek to progress. They remain where they are because it is convenient and where they are most effective place to sell them the maximum number of illusions.

Now, as a result, people are in a state of constant frustration, because they perceive their own mediocrity. They well understand that they have stopped progressing, and this frustration is converted into beer, consumer products and endless other things that fill them. Thus, they remain stuck at the same level, still they create for themselves the illusion that they have truly accomplished something—that they have progressed.

This illusion is created, amongst other things, by the activity of shopping. Psychologically, as many studies have shown, shopping is a great way to forget about everything. We walk around the mall, certain that everything is within our reach. When we purchase something, we immediately feel we've moved ahead. Here, we finally got the gadget we've always dreamed of, that is, since that ad got stuck in our subconscious.

The corporations are aware of this power they wield

and these feelings they produce in their consumers. It is in their best interest that we get stuck, that we become depressed, that we try to lift our depression via shopping sprees or by taking anti-depressant pills that are sold like water. But, the moment we buy, we are just digging ourselves a deeper hole, because eventually we will discover by how much our debt has really grown, and then the real depression will set in.

The summary is that we have no freedom of choice. We are put on track nearly from the moment we are born. We feel proud of our children when they successfully identify the logos of various companies, and we encourage them to "choose" the brand names they want to wear, as each brand name "comments on" their character, personality and lifestyle. Often, we buy them the most expensive brand names ourselves, though, personally, I have yet to meet a little boy who cares whether his first pair of shoes are Adidas or not.

So, we act so as to give an advantage to corporations and vest our illusion of choice in the next generation, which grows up thinking that brand names and fancy things have significance. At this point, corporations needn't invest as much as they did before. They already have a captive audience. For example, the "families" of

Apple, who will purchase every fart the company produces just because its logo is printed on the package.

So, yes, you can fool everyone all the time. Till now.

EPILOGUE

Very soon I estimate that democracies of the world will cease to exist as we know them. They will disappear, because there is no other option. Because the system has stopped working. Because the corporations are the almighty rulers of our daily reality. The democracies will be replaced, just like every other form of governance in the past has been replaced, when they stop serving the powers that be.

I believe that the election of Trump is a sign of the coming tipping point. If you study what has happened throughout the 2016 presidential election you should be able to identify two forces. The first—for the first time in the modern history of democracies, in which money was always in the back controlling politicians as puppets on strings—is the Hubris hitting the roof. Billionaires are moving to the front and seating themselves in the ruling chairs. The second, although Trump in his inauguration said he is going to "make America great again," is the hidden truth that American corporations, which have lost power in the past twenty to thirty years, due to the success of China and other competitors, put Trump in control to "make America's corporations great again."

I believe these are only initial signs of great movements of powers that to come in the following years, in which a new system will evolve that enables the powers that be to rule.

But, the moment we, the masses, awaken and understand these processes, the truly great movement of change will start. When this happens, the real battle shall begin—not between Hillary and Trump, not between Apple and Microsoft. Between us and them.

There is talk of a direct democracy or of other forms of governance emerging. Will the nations of the world unite to form a corporate UN that embraces moral rules, corporate ethics and a punitive mechanism based on revoking corporations' patents and intellectual property? It is too early to know what will happen and which systems will succeed. But one thing is certain: the moment the masses shake themselves awake from the misleading consciousness of consumerism culture, of being bonded by debt, something will happen. Whether by lighting fires, setting barricades or performing peaceful demonstrations, something will happen.

We must remember...

The corporate souls will try everything to prevent this seizure of power. They will fight. At first, they will try insincerely praise the public in order to persuade us to continue buying. Then, they will try the divide-and-rule method by literally buying the leaders of the revolution, as has happened many times before throughout history. But this kind of revolution willn't have and needn't have leaders. It must grow from the grassroots, from the masses. And when the masses sober up and smarten up, it will be impossible to buy us off.

The beginning and end of the revolution is determined by our consumer habits. There is no way we can be forced to open our wallets and buy. Corporations, ads, television—these actors can attempt to persuade us, to brainwash us. But we cannot be forced. The moment we reach a decision and stop, the revolution will begin.

"People of the world unite. You have nothing to lose but your digital chains to debt."